Thinking Catholic

ALSO BY ARCHBISHOP DANIEL E. PILARCZYK

Lenten Lunches:
   Reflections on the Weekday Readings
   for Lent and Easter Week

Living in the Lord:
   The Building Blocks of Spirituality

Twelve Tough Issues:
   What the Church Teaches—and Why

What Must I Do?
   Morality and the Challenge of God's Word

Thinking
Catholic

Archbishop Daniel E. Pilarczyk

ST. ANTHONY MESSENGER PRESS

Cincinnati, Ohio

Scripture citations are taken from the *New American Bible With Revised New Testament*, copyright ©1986, by the Confraternity of Christian Doctrine (CCD), Washington, D.C., and are used with permission. All rights reserved.

Cover photograph by Gene Plaisted, O.S.C.
Cover design by Karla Ann Sheppard
Book design by Mary Alfieri
Electronic pagination and format by Sandy L. Digman

ISBN 0-86716-327-5

Published by St. Anthony Messenger Press
Printed in the U.S.A.

Contents

Introduction

This series of reflections has its origin in a conversation I had with one of our priests of the Archdiocese of Cincinnati some time ago. We were discussing the practice of the faith among our people, and we recalled that, according to survey statistics, the incidence of birth control and abortion and divorce among Catholics isn't much less than among the American population at large. I mentioned that lots of Catholics don't seem to see much wrong in homosexual genital activity. He said he knew an apparently devout Catholic woman who said she hoped that assisted suicide would become legal soon so that, when her time came, she wouldn't have to linger at length and cause problems for her family.

He then said he thought that many of our people have not been properly educated. They don't know what the Church teaches about these matters or, if they know, they don't find the arguments for the teachings to be convincing—at least not convincing enough to make them follow the teachings.

I admitted that he might be right. I recalled that we both know some good Catholic families who had sent their children to Catholic schools for eight, twelve or sixteen years and now the children have either lost the faith entirely or are marginalized Catholics. Yet we also know other good Catholic families who provided the same kind of formal education and now the adult children and their children are loyal and enthusiastic practicing Catholics. Knowledge alone doesn't seem to be the issue.

It is clear that the world around us doesn't give the kind of support to Catholic Christian belief and behavior that it once did, and that living a Christian life is therefore harder than it used to be.

In our American society people used to agree without a second thought that abortion was criminal, that divorce was bad, that sexual activity outside of marriage was wrong, that homosexual behavior was not natural. Today all of these things are not only acceptable in our culture but are looked upon as rights that no one can take away. That's the message that is conveyed to us over and over again in popular music, movies and TV programs. All we have to do is read the daily papers (and their advertisements) to realize that the values many people hold are not Christian values such as self-sacrifice and patience and obedience to the will of the Lord.

Our American society is dedicated to consumption. We are bombarded with invitations to buy, to enjoy, to use up, to throw away and then to buy again. While many voices tell us why to buy certain products, there seem to be few voices that tell us the purpose of all this buying and using up. Our whole country seems to be engaged in an activity that nobody can really justify. It's an exercise in futility.

Equally futile are many of the commonly accepted ideas about success, work, comfort, education and human relationships.

From the point of view of a believer, none of it makes much sense. The world seems to have gone crazy.

If we are to maintain our Catholic Christian faith in the midst of all this madness, we have to be able to maintain our equilibrium. We have to have something inside of us that helps us keep our balance when everything around us seems to be sliding toward dissolution.

Knowledge is important. We need to know what God expects of us and why. We need to understand that the real demands of our faith are not the whims of a difficult God, but guidance about authentic growth and development. But knowledge alone does not seem to be enough.

The early Greek philosopher Socrates thought that nobody ever does evil willingly, but only because he or she is badly informed. If people really knew what was right, he maintained, they would never do wrong. Subsequent reflection has rejected this position, now known as the Socratic fallacy. People know what is right, but they do wrong anyway because the wrong seems more immediately appealing or profitable, or because the reasons given for avoiding wrongdoing don't seem to be persuasive in all circumstances.

Knowledge is important, but it is not enough. If it were, straight A's in religion and theology courses ought to guarantee faithfulness and virtue, but they don't. Something more than knowledge seems to be called for.

This "something more" is what I call "thinking

Catholic." Thinking Catholic is not just a matter of knowing what Christ and his Church teach, even in detail. Thinking Catholic is a mindset, an attitude of the heart, a bundle of insights and presumptions and priorities and directions that are derived from faith and which, in turn, strengthen and vitalize the practice of faith. Catholic thinking is like a hidden file in a computer program that may never appear on the screen but that governs the whole operation of the program. If it is not there, things just are not going to work.

The people who think Catholic are those who are able to maintain their sense of equilibrium in a crazy world. Those who do not are sucked into the whirlpool, no matter how much they may have been taught about the specifics of Catholic faith and practice.

These insights, presumptions and priorities that lie in the heart of the faithful believer are concerned with God and the world, with life and living, with suffering and sin, with the individual and the family and with society at large. They involve our attitudes toward happiness, toward knowledge and the arts, toward the inconsistencies of human existence. Thinking Catholic includes our attitudes toward Christ and prayer and the Church.

Thinking Catholic is not something we can outline with completeness and detail because it contains so many elements and because it is as complex as the human heart. It is a mixture of motivating forces that may vary from individual to individual, but that includes some essential features common to all faithful believers. It is not a collection of separate items like tools in a tool box, but rather a blend of energies, each of which influences the others, like the various flavors in good wine.

In the chapters that follow I offer a description of thinking Catholic. I use the word *description* deliberately because I am sure that others would be able to find other aspects of the Catholic mindset or explain differently the ones I present. I will deal with what I perceive.

I will treat the elements of thinking Catholic that have to do with the world around us, then those concerned with our life and how we live it. I will then have something to say about aspects of thinking Catholic that govern our relationship with the Church and our religious practice.

My purpose is not polemic. I have not set out to demonstrate how crazy and how bad things are in the world that surrounds us. There isn't much need for such a demonstration. Those who need to be convinced that things are not what they should be have only to consider the frenzy and the frustration of the world's "successful" people to see that the world promises more than it can deliver, that its sales pitch is tinged with madness.

My purpose is to clarify the Catholic heart and the Catholic mind to show how deeply different we are—or should be—from many of those around us. It is my hope that becoming aware of what lies within the heart of those who think Catholic will enable those who read these reflections to become aware of the richness that both derives from our faith and also energizes it. This awareness may be of some assistance in staying faithful in a crazy world. I will be content if these reflections help people to savor and appreciate and nourish the gift of thinking Catholic.

CHAPTER ONE

A Wonderful World

How we look on the world pretty well determines how we see everything else in our lives. If we see the world as a result of some cosmic fluke, we will see our own lives as fundamentally meaningless, to be lived out as comfortably and pleasantly as we can make them until the time comes for the end of our absurd existence. If we see the world as a grim and desolate place, we will expect to lead grim and desolate lives. If we see the world as a place of trial and temptation in which God is constantly exercising quality control over the creatures that have been placed here, we will see everything as threat and live our lives in cowering fear. If we see the world exclusively as a vale of tears, we will see everything as a cause for lamentation.

Most people don't seem to give much thought to the nature and meaning of the universe. They leave such questions to scientists and philosophers. Instead, they take life as it comes, one day at a time, pursuing their various inclinations and generally following the path of least resistance. But in living that way, they are nonetheless implicitly saying something about their view of the world. They are saying that it really isn't very important, just as their own lives are unimportant to anyone beyond themselves and their immediate circle of human contacts.

The best way to look at the world is through the eyes of the One who put it here in the first place. At the beginning of the Bible, we learn that God thinks the world is good. In the creation narrative in Genesis (1:1—2:4) we see God calling the world out of nothingness. The work is planned and careful, and God is pleased with it. Not fewer than seven times in that first chapter do we read that God looked on what he had created and saw that it was good: light, water and dry land, vegetation, the sun and the moon, fish and birds and cattle and reptiles, human beings. In God's eyes it's all good—very good.

Whatever else may have happened since then, whatever we shortsighted human beings may have done to God's skilled handiwork, the world started out good, and not even we are bad enough to ruin the goodness that God laid down at its foundation.

There has been much speculation over the centuries about *how* God created the world. People used to think that each species of animal and plant was specifically and individually created by God. Now we are more inclined to think that God created a process, a process that may have started eight or ten billion years ago and has been unfolding ever since. Whatever we may think about such matters, it is clear that the Book of Genesis is not intended to be a scientific treatise about *how* the world was created. It is rather a religious book about *who* and *what*. It is God who is the source of the world, and what God created was and is good.

Genesis is also about *why*. God created the world for

2

the same reason that human beings write poetry and sing songs: He wanted to express himself. Given the right circumstances, each of us likes to say who and what we are, to speak our heart. It's the same with God. God expresses himself in this world of ours, and what God expresses is goodness. God created the world because God is good and wanted others to share in that goodness. And wanting to share goodness is another name for love.

God created the world out of love because he wanted to express his goodness and share it with stars and planets, with palm trees and morning glory vines, with cows and pigs, and, yes, even with us.

One of the prominent scientists of our time has said that we are such insignificant creatures on a minor planet of an average star at the outer suburbs of a hundred thousand million galaxies that it's difficult to believe in a God who would care about us or even notice our existence. In my opinion, that's faulty logic. The fact that creation is bigger than we once thought doesn't mean that God is any less involved in it. It simply means that our idea of God has probably been too limited. It's not at all difficult to believe that God notices our existence or cares about us, no matter how big his creation may be, if God is our loving Creator. We are always insignificant and unimportant in comparison with God, but God doesn't love us because of our significance or importance. God loves us because God is God.

Of course there is pain and suffering in the world, and we'll be saying something more about that later. Some of it comes of our own doing and that of human

3

beings who have lived before us. Some of it seems meaningless and cruel. But even that doesn't mean that God is cruel or that creation is inherently flawed. It means that God's love for creation is so great that he is able to express and bring about goodness even when we can't understand how.

We live in a great and good and wonderful creation. We're just beginning to find out how vast it is, and we haven't come close to learning about or appreciating the little corner of it that God has given to us to enjoy. And it all runs on God's love.

Thinking Catholic involves a hard-headed, objective and loving appreciation of God's work of creation. The world is not an accident, not a dungeon, not just a vale of tears (even though we sometimes have done our best to make it that). The world is God's doing, created with a purpose, and that purpose is to let others share in divine goodness and love.

At the same time, thinking Catholic does not mean overlooking the real suffering and evil in the world. These things are there and we are called to do something about them. But suffering and evil are only the ground clutter on the weather map of God's work. Above the ground clutter is God's perspective on the world. God sees it today as God saw it at the end of that first work of creation. It was very good then and it is very good now.

That's why thinking Catholic involves radical optimism. It's not inappropriate to be concerned about war and poverty and disease. It's not bad to be distressed about drug abuse and divorce and rampant selfishness. Thinking Catholic does not mean denying that we live in a crazy world. But however crazy the world may be, it is still God's world, it is still a good world, and, no matter what else happens, God's love still makes the world go round.

If we are going to keep ourselves attuned to the fundamental reality and meaning of God's world, it's important to exercise regular and conscious appreciation of it, to acknowledge the beauty of the sunset, the freshness of a summer breeze, the wonder of dinosaur bones buried in a desert, the mind-boggling multiplicity of the stars, the seemingly infinite variety of earthly plants and animals. (I have subscribed to *National Geographic* for a long time. I find it helps me be attentive to the magnificence of God's world.)

We also need to reflect on and be grateful for the gifts that God has put into human minds and hearts: gifts of expression in words and stone and paint and music, gifts of thought and insight, gifts of self-sacrifice and affection. God's wisdom and goodness and love are imprinted all over this world of ours. The wise and faithful person is the one who knows how to recognize them and rejoice in them.

How we look on the world determines how we see everything else. Thinking Catholic involves recognizing the world as the canticle of God's goodness and love and being willing to sing along.

CHAPTER TWO

Guests at God's Celebration

The world that God created does not belong to us. It belongs to God. We are guests here, invited for a temporary stay while permanent arrangements are being made for us. But while we are here, God has plans for us.

To begin with, God wants us to enjoy what he has created. God wants us to have a good time at this celebration of his goodness and love. The vastness and variety and beauty of what God has created are intended to give pleasure not just to him, but to us as well. God doesn't mean for us to be wallflowers at the celebration, waiting quietly until it's time to go home. God means for us to be part of what's going on. He wants us to relish the sights and sounds that he has put here for us. God wants us to mingle with the other guests and to derive pleasure from their company. It's OK to laugh and talk and sing along with the music. It's OK to applaud. It's OK to "ooh" and "aah" at the gifts that God gives his guests. It's OK to encourage others to enjoy them with us. To do otherwise would be to imply that God didn't do a very good job in expressing himself in creation. Enchantment with the wonder of God's creation is one of the qualities that make people like Saint Francis of Assisi so attractive.

Of course we have to enjoy the celebration appropriately. It's God's party, not ours. We are guests in somebody else's home. We are not free to take over what God has provided for us and turn it to purposes that God didn't intend. Unfortunately, we seem to be pretty good at doing just that. Right from the beginning the first human participants in the celebration tried to take it over and push God out of the way. They wanted to be hosts rather than guests, masters of the household rather than visitors.

People have been doing the same thing ever since. We take God's gift of speech, for example, and use it to hurt others. We take the strength and ingenuity that God has given us and use it to make wars or to impose injustice on others. Sometimes it seems as if the whole party has gotten out of hand and we are involved in a pagan orgy rather than a godly celebration.

At one point, the world got so bad that God sent his own Son to get things back on track. Jesus came to announce the coming of the Kingdom of God, a state in which everything is under God's loving control once more and the party restored to sanity. One of the images that Jesus liked to use to describe the Kingdom was a banquet, an ordered gathering in which everybody is having a good time. The Kingdom began with Jesus and is still with us. The celebration and the sharing of God's goodness and love hasn't ended. It's still going on despite the misbehavior of the guests. Creation is still good and God still intends us to enjoy it.

But there's more. God doesn't mean for us just to be grateful spectators or passive recipients in the celebration. He wants us to contribute to it. One of the most important gifts that God has given us is the gift of sharing in his creativity.

God has enabled us to take the raw materials of creation and turn them into medicines and statues and automobiles and houses and computers. God has given us the capacity to discover the complexity and beauty of creation and to share our discoveries with others in words and pictures and music. God has gifted us with the ability to learn how to grow crops and raise animals and even make whole new varieties of living things for our well-being and enjoyment. What God saw as good in the beginning was only the beginning. Much more has happened since then because of God's invitation to us to participate in the creative celebration.

Most important of all, God has invited and enabled us to participate in the creation of ourselves. We begin as helpless infants, dependent on others for everything. But as time goes by, we begin to make decisions and choices for ourselves. Those decisions and choices, based on the potential that God has given to each of us, gradually determine what we become. The helpless infant becomes a rocket scientist or a farmer or a doctor or a concert violinist or a priest. The dependent baby grows up to become a parent, passing on and shaping the gift of life in new human beings.

We can use the potential that God has given us to turn into thoughtful and generous human beings. We can be men and women who are grateful and attentive to God, consciously aware of the goodness and love around us. It all depends on how we use the capacities that God has given us to participate in the celebration.

That's not to say it's easy. Making good choices can be very demanding, thanks to our limited perspective and the selfishness that comes with our fallen human nature. We create ourselves a little bit at a time. Becoming a good human being takes at least as much effort and practice as becoming an Olympic athlete.

Sometimes we are inclined to give up and just drift along. But when we do that, we are letting circumstances or other people make our decisions for us. To refuse to expend the effort to make ourselves something beautiful for God is to opt out of our part in the celebration.

In June 1996 in Cincinnati we observed the one hundred and seventy-fifth anniversary of the foundation of our diocese with a solemn liturgy of thanksgiving. The clergy and religious and laypeople of the archdiocese were invited as well as others who had been connected with our local church over the years. There were all kinds of committees to look after the invitations, the comfort of the guests from outside the diocese, the planning of the anniversary liturgy, the music and the reception outside the cathedral afterward. Lots of people worked very hard to bring the event to a successful outcome. It was a wonderful celebration and it was no less a celebration because of the planning and effort that it required. In fact, those who had helped bring the celebration about experienced a level of satisfaction beyond that of the guests.

Our contribution to God's celebration of goodness and love does indeed require persistence and patience and effort. But it's still celebration.

Thinking Catholic involves conscious participation in God's celebration. We are not in a prison in which we wait for our sentence to be ended so that we can leave. We are at a party, and God means for us to have a good time and help others have a good time, too.

Of course our life on this earth is not a period of mindless hilarity. Life is serious business, and God wants us to take it seriously. But the seriousness is not the seriousness of enduring a punishment. It's the seriousness of effort to make our contribution to the celebration. Life is not a burden to be borne but a gift to be appreciated and responded to.

Those who think Catholic know that it is good to be alive. They take pleasure in the gifts that God has provided for them. They are grateful. They are also attentive to the capabilities that God has given them to make the celebration even better. They are not content just to listen to the music. They are also anxious to perform as skillfully as they can the particular part that God has assigned to them.

CHAPTER THREE

Our Host Is With Us

It would be a strange host who gave a party and didn't show up personally or who appeared at the beginning to get things started and then disappeared. We expect our host to be around during a celebration, not only to see that the guests are well attended to, but also to take part in the party.

God is a good host. God didn't set up the celebration of his goodness and love and then walk away, intending to return at the end to turn off the lights and clean up the mess. No, God is part of the celebration, present and active at every phase. Thinking Catholic involves being aware of our host and being able to recognize him, not only to reassure ourselves that he is still around, but also to learn from him what is going on and how we are expected to respond.

There are many ways to see God in creation. Everything that *is* is somehow created to reflect God. We can see the power of God in the thunderstorm and the immensity of God in the sky and the sea. A cat licking her kittens shows us something about God's tenderness. The seemingly limitless variety of plants is an indication of the generosity of God who was not content to create just a few species, but thousands and thousands for our use and enjoyment. When we enter the realm of the human, the images of God are even more varied. Tall people and short people, creative people and plodding people, people with gifts of affectivity and people with gifts of logic and mental discipline, people who talk and laugh a lot and people who are quiet and reserved—all of them reflect something about God.

Of course the imprint of God isn't always obvious—it's hard to see God in a cockroach. But God's imprint is there somewhere. For that matter, finding God in a rose or a sunset is not inevitable unless we are willing to look for him there. God's imprint in creation is like one of those puzzles in the Sunday paper that appear to be a meaningless jumble of colors and lines until we look at it in a certain way and come to recognize the picture that is there. Part of thinking Catholic is knowing how to look at the picture.

But God's presence at the celebration is not limited to imprints and images left behind for us to look at. God is also personally present and active in what's going on here.

For one thing, God's power and therefore God's presence is active just in keeping things going. If God were to withdraw his love and attention from creation for even a moment, all the countless galaxies with their stars and planets (including little Earth off in the outer suburbs) would simply lapse back into nothingness. The simple fact that things *are* indicates that God is around somewhere. If he weren't, there would be nothing.

But that's not all. If God has enabled and invited us human beings to participate in and contribute to the celebration, and if we can only be and act through the power and the presence of the Creator, then our interaction with one another is also a manifestation of the presence of God. A mother's care for her child, a husband's concern for his wife, the affection of friends for one another, a priest's dedication to his people—all are ultimately actions of God who is there in them all.

Sometimes it's hard to see the presence and action of God in what people do to one another. Is God active in the child abuser and the war criminal? Yes, at least insofar as he has given these people life and some basic human capabilities. The difficulty in seeing God arises from the misuse and distortion to which these persons have turned God's presence in them. The challenge is to be willing to look behind the evil and see that even this cannot totally obliterate the godliness that lies deep inside.

But the presence of God goes beyond anonymous action in maintaining the world and in enabling human beings to do good for one another. God is also in touch with us directly and in his own name.

We Christians believe that God speaks to us in the Bible. These narratives of kings and prophets and miracles, these collections of wise sayings, these letters and visions from long ago are God's word to us. God is in them as much as we are in the words we speak to one another. Their meaning for us here and now is not always obvious. God has not chosen to address us in words and images that a child can understand completely. This may be because the truth God wants to communicate to us is more complex than that, or because he wants us to have to exert some effort to grasp the meaning so that we will understand it better.

Yet the fact remains that the Lord is present in his word.

The Lord is also present in the community of believers that we call Church. The risen Jesus promised to be with this community forever, to love its members through their love for one another, to protect them in time of trial. Catholics look on the Church as the Body of Christ, a body whose soul is the Holy Spirit, a body whose activity is the ongoing activity of Christ.

In the context of the Church, God is most intensely present in the sacraments. Every time one of the sacraments is celebrated, God the Father acts in Christ his Son through the Holy Spirit: to begin his life in us, to forgive our sins, to strengthen us in times of illness, to make us extensions of his love in marriage or ordained ministry. The capstone of the sacraments, of course, is the Holy Eucharist in which Christ himself, personally and really, comes to nourish our life in him and to make his presence accessible to us as friend and brother.

The master of the celebration is indeed with us. In fact, like a good host, God is all over the place, in countless ways, in countless manifestations. Yet he is a polite host who doesn't impose himself on his guests at every moment, who doesn't intrude himself on what they may be engaged in. He waits to be recognized.

Thinking Catholic means being able to recognize and appreciate the presence of God in our lives. This is something a little different from knowing about God or acknowledging God's authority and power. It involves consciously being with God.

This requires practice. We have to form the habit of looking for God, of searching out his presence in nature, in other people and in our own hearts. We have to keep calling ourselves to attentiveness to him even when we listen to Sacred Scripture or participate in the celebration of the sacraments.

We seem to suffer from a sort of natural nearsightedness and superficiality, probably due to our inherited inclination to sin. We are fascinated with the immediate and the obvious, with our own personal needs and wants. It takes a little effort to accustom ourselves to look beyond all that.

When I was in the seminary and it was prayer time, the prayer leader would always say, "Let us put ourselves into the presence of God." It was an invitation to refocus, to leave some of our baggage behind, to close off the noise, to look toward different horizons and to open ourselves to the Lord. Yet we don't have to be at formal, organized prayer in order to put ourselves into the presence of God. We can accustom ourselves to doing it in just about every aspect of our life: when we get up in the morning, as we start our work, when we begin our meals, when we meet a friend, even when we are just walking down the street. We can always put ourselves into the presence of God because God is always present in one way or another.

Thinking Catholic means living our life in awareness of the company of our host.

CHAPTER FOUR

Life on Loan

People who don't know much at all about Catholic thinking do know that Catholics are against abortion and assisted suicide. If they are a little better informed they know that Catholic teaching is also opposed to artificial contraception and test-tube babies. Since all of these things are more or less accepted in our society, the general public sometimes looks on the Catholic position on these matters as old-fashioned, at best quaint and at worst socially divisive. Why don't Catholics get with it and join the modern world? Why don't they change their rules and stop making trouble for society at large?

The Catholic position on these matters is not a set of laws laid down by Church leaders. It is a direct consequence of thinking Catholic about the most fundamental elements of human existence.

Creation is the expression of God's goodness and love, a celebration in which human beings are called to share and an ongoing process to which human beings are called to contribute. It's God's show, not ours, and individual human life is not a possession that we have been given to use as we see fit, but an instrument that God loans us to enable us to carry out our part in his plans.

Moreover, of all the gifts that God has entrusted to us, our life is the most basic because life is the fundamental condition of the process of human existence. It's not just one faculty among many, like speech or thought. Human life is the vehicle for everything else, the operating system on which all God's programs run.

All human life belongs to God—my life and the life of every other human being, past, present and future. And all human life is given for God's purposes. This is the fundamental insight that distinguishes thinking Catholic from much of the craziness of the rest of the world.

If human life is given to us on loan to use for God's purposes, then it is not right for me to end my human life when I see fit. To do so is to opt out of the celebration, to indicate that I want no further part in what is going on in creation, that I want to leave the party before my part in it is completed.

Likewise, if each human life is a unique gift from God, it is not right for me to take the life of another human being, whether it be the life of a personal enemy or a convicted criminal, of a sick friend or an unborn child. It's not up to us to interfere in the plans that God may have for other people.

Again, if human life is given as a gift of God and for God's purposes, it is not right to do as we please with the processes by which human life comes into being. To try to bring human beings into existence exclusively in accord with our wishes and our convenience, to try to have children born according to our specifications constitutes interference with one of the most basic acts of the Creator.

When we tamper in these ways with human life, we are not only abusing our privileges as guests at God's celebration. We are, in effect, trying to take over the celebration by controlling the guest list. It is a particularly extreme attempt to oust the host and put ourselves in his place.

This is all part of thinking Catholic. Much of the world around us would say that if Catholics want to think that way, they are free to do so, as long as they allow other people to do as they see fit in these matters. But it's not that simple.

Abusing human life is not just a matter of acting in disaccord with a given religious mind-set. It also brings natural and inevitable consequences of its own. You can't interfere with the way things are made to be and not expect something else to go wrong.

When people decide, as many in our crazy world have decided, that human life is a personal possession, ours to do with as we see fit, they open the door to all sorts of unexpected horrors. If suicide is acceptable, then why should I ever endure hardships and pain and struggle of any sort? Why not just end it all today? If it is acceptable to help a sick relative commit suicide when that person's life is too burdensome to him or her, what is wrong with persuading that person to commit suicide when his or her life is too burdensome to me?

If it is acceptable to terminate the life of an unborn child when that life seems to threaten its mother, why can it be wrong to end the unborn life that is merely inconvenient? For that matter, what's wrong with ending the life of a child already born if the child is more than the parents think they can handle? (We have already reached the point in our society where it is legally acceptable to kill a partially born child.) Once people have accepted the idea of custom-made children, conceived according to the timetable and the description specified by the parents—or parent—how is the child different from other objects that we can order up according to our individual desires?

Human experience in these last few decades, both here in the United States and elsewhere, seems to be teaching us that treating human life as a possession creates more problems than it is intended to solve. Some thinking people, even those who do not think Catholic, are beginning to see that human society can survive only if human life is held inviolable, universally protected by government and beyond the reach of private individuals. Human beings are simply not equipped to be in arbitrary control of human life.

Of course people don't interfere with human life—their own or that of others—because they want to destroy human society. They do so because human life can be painful, frustrating and difficult.

From the perspective of public policy, the response to these realities ought to be that, in spite of the pain and frustration and difficulty, it is still better in the long run to keep our hands off human life because of the terrible things that seem to happen when we begin to interfere with it. We simply don't know enough to be in charge.

Thinking Catholic provides a more reassuring perspective. We don't deny the pain and effort that is part of every human life. But we are also aware that

God's view and ours are sometimes different. We tend to be shortsighted and think that there is something wrong with a life that is not pleasant or productive here and now. God doesn't look only at the here and now. God looks at the life of each of us in the light of the contribution that it makes to the plan of creation, the plan of goodness and love in which we participate. We don't have to understand everything. We can't, any more than children can understand why they have to go to the dentist. God is good enough and wise enough to bring benefit to his creation and blessing to us even out of terminal cancer and deformed children and total human failure.

Thinking Catholic includes the conviction that God knows what he is doing in each of us, that he uses the basic instrument that he has loaned to us, our individual human life, for purposes that surpass our immediate awareness. It's not for us to destroy or tamper with the instrument because we happen not to understand what God is doing with it. Unqualified respect for the gift of life is an essential component of thinking Catholic.

CHAPTER FIVE

A Happy Ending

S ometimes it's hard to believe that this world we share is really God's world, and still harder to believe that it is a celebration of goodness and love. Sin and pain and frustration and evil are everywhere.

We are all personally acquainted with sickness and struggle. Disappointment is part of everybody's life. Sometimes it seems that, no matter how hard we try, things just don't seem to turn out right. Inside each of us are inclinations toward selfishness and sin which, in our better moments, we know are invitations to greater or lesser degrees of self-destruction. Acquiring bad habits is easy, and rooting them out is hard. Whole schools of philosophy have looked on these realities and concluded that our individual human life is an exercise in frustration, meaninglessness or boredom.

Things are not much better when we look on human history as a whole. We have come a long way from the Stone Age to the computer age. We presently enjoy comforts and capabilities that were beyond our great-grandparents' imagination. Yet in other ways we are worse off than we were before. Values of family life that most people once took for granted are disappearing. It seems that the education of our young people has degenerated into damage control. New sicknesses have arisen that we are unable to control. Economic betterment for some seems necessarily connected with impoverishment for others. We have still not found ways to resolve human conflicts. The wars of the past seem almost humane compared with the armed struggles of our own lifetime and with the destructive capabilities that we have prepared for the future. We have now reached a point where we are likely to destroy the world itself if we are not careful, and we don't have a very good track record in guarding against destruction.

In view of all that, this world and this life may not seem like much of a celebration. They seem more like a catastrophe, an exercise in pointlessness or, at best, a good plan that has gone awry and whose ending can only be destruction when God has finally grown tired of it.

Thinking Catholic helps us see things differently. There is no denying the reality of evil. It is real. It is destructive. But those who think Catholic know that human selfishness, blindness and destructiveness are not going to be the last word. We live in hope, in the conviction that better things lie ahead and that God is good enough and wise enough and powerful enough to bring his good plans to fulfillment in spite of all the ingenuity and willfulness of the human heart.

If God had intended to write off creation as a bad job, he has had every chance to do so over the millennia of human history. But that's not what God did. Instead he sent his Son to start over, to institute a new creation that lives in Christ and that will live and grow as long as

Christ is with us—and he promised to be with us forever. This new creation will conclude when Christ comes in glory to take all that is good in creation to himself in the final stage of the Kingdom of God.

Jesus is everything that God ever intended humanity to be. And what Jesus came to be and to do will determine the final form and the final fulfillment of creation. It will all somehow be like him when he gathers it to himself in the Kingdom.

Jesus made it quite clear that we don't need to understand how that's going to come about, still less when it's going to happen. But he has promised that it will be so. Thinking Catholic means taking him at his word.

But the final saving of creation, its victory over all the viciousness of human self-will, is not something that Christ Jesus is going to bring about all alone. The drama of God's love doesn't have just one hero, but a whole cast of them. Jesus invites each of us to be in that cast.

In the shorthand terminology of thinking Catholic we speak of heaven and hell. Good people end up in heaven for all eternity, bad people in hell. Sometimes we oversimplify and find ourselves thinking about heaven and hell as places, and about the process of getting there as a kind of bookkeeping operation in which God totals up the accounts of good and evil in the life of each of us and comes up with a closing balance that determines where we go.

There's some truth in that, but the reality is a little more complex. God doesn't just give us a series of tests to pass in order to squeak into heaven. Rather, God invites us to work with him in the salvation of creation.

God gives us a share in the life of Christ when we are baptized, and we spend the rest of our life responding to that gift.

If we are faithful to our calling to continue the life and mission of Christ, we gradually grow more and more into the Kingdom. We are more and more conscious of the goodness and love of God. We are more and more eager to share that goodness and love with the people around us, sometimes in big ways, sometimes in little ways, sometimes at the cost of great sacrifice, sometimes through acts of kindness and consideration that are almost automatic. Through our life Christ's Kingdom grows a little stronger in the world and we ourselves grow more and more at home in the presence of the Lord, more and more at one with God's ways of seeing and doing. When our life reaches its conclusion, we continue living as we have lived before, only now it is in the fully revealed presence of God. We "go to heaven," not because of some final decision on God's part, but because of what we have become in our years of earthly collaboration with God's celebration of goodness and love. God doesn't merely decide to let us in. It's where we belong.

Those who reject God's offer to collaborate in his plans drift farther and farther away from the purpose of creation. They center themselves on secondary or destructive things, sometimes through consciously-made big decisions, sometimes through a series of smaller, less conscious ones that gradually eat away at their connection with God until they themselves determine that participating in God's plans is no longer important. Instead of working to bring the Kingdom of

Christ closer in themselves and in others, they impede its growth.

Finally, when there are no more choices to be made, they find that all that is left is the Kingdom of heaven or eternal detachment from it. Since they have spent their lives walking away from the Kingdom, all that is left for them is to be a failure forever, an eternal outsider. God has not created hell as a place where he can put bad people. People create hell for themselves and put themselves in it by their rejection and destruction of what God had in mind for them.

Thinking Catholic doesn't mean trying to believe that sick people are not sick or that human suffering is merely an illusion or that human sinfulness is of no consequence. Thinking Catholic does not mean trying to convince ourselves that everything is really all right here and now. Everything is not all right here and now, and there is no point in pretending otherwise. But thinking Catholic does involve the conviction that somehow, sometime things will be all right, even if we can't understand how. Thinking Catholic involves the awareness of the power of the continuing life of Christ and of God's invitation to us to share that life forever.

Thinking Catholic means being realistic enough to look forward to a happy ending.

CHAPTER SIX

It All Depends

Maturity involves a sense of proportion. I suspect that most of us have had the experience of feeling that the world was going to come to an end because of something we did or something that happened to us. We did badly on an exam at school, we said something that we immediately knew was a terrible gaffe, we got sick and couldn't go to the party we had been looking forward to, we had a flat tire on the way to a job interview.

Our first reaction was to think that life was over for us, that the world held no further joy, that we would be better off dead. Then time passed and the world went on in spite of what had happened. Soon we picked up where we left off and found that there was still life ahead of us.

In retrospect, we may now even be able to discover some good that came of what seemed like catastrophe. We begin to see the thing in a different perspective. We grow up a little bit and our sense of proportion deepens. That terrible thing was relative to our stage of personal development and to the circumstances of the moment.

Thinking Catholic, which is another name for Christian maturity, involves an awareness of how much in our life is relative: relative to our capacity to understand and endure it, relative to our state of mind, relative to the goals and values that guide our lives. Our life doesn't become worthless or meaningless because of anything that happens to us or even because of anything we do to ourselves. It all depends on what we make of it, on the way it fits in with God's enduring love and care for us.

What's important in our lives is not so much *what* happens as *how we deal* with the events: the direction in which we choose to orient them, the value and the meaning that we find in them. This is true whether what happens is something that seems good or bad.

Most people would be glad to be so wealthy that they never have to worry about money again. There's nothing wrong with that, but the real significance of wealth for a person's life depends on what the person does with these resources. Using wealth to ride roughshod over others, to demand attention, to set oneself up in mindless comfort and needless consumption is one thing. Using wealth as a means to help others and make God's goodness more immediate for them is something else.

The greatest human achievements can be turned into self-indulgence and even misery if they are not properly oriented, while "ordinary" human success, like holding down a decent job and raising a family, can bring a degree of happiness that more conspicuously "successful" people might never enjoy. It all depends. What matters is what you do with it.

It's the same with trials and sufferings. Some people emerge from suffering with a deepened sense of the meaning of their lives, with gratitude and appreciation for what they have experienced. Others emerge broken and embittered. It all depends on what you do with it.

Developing an appropriate understanding of what happens in our lives is difficult for us human beings because we tend to be so childish and so nearsighted. If it feels good, we just want to sit back and enjoy it without bothering to find out what else is involved and what responsibilities may be associated with it. If it feels bad, we want to fix it immediately so that the hurt will go away, regardless of what else may be involved. We tend to absolutize both pleasure and pain, whereas both depend for their meaning on other, far more important matters.

Whether we feel good or bad is not of primary importance. Whether we are a success or a failure as the world counts success and failure is not what matters. What really matters is how our lives fit into our role in God's plan of goodness and love. Everything else depends on that.

In this context we might do well to reflect on the life and death of Jesus. By any merely human standards, Jesus' life was a failure. He didn't get much recognition from important people. The men and women who did follow him were not prominent or powerful. Some of his followers were significantly unimpressive. In the end he was scorned and derided and put to death by one of the most painful methods that human ingenuity has been able to devise. From one perspective, all this was an insignificant episode in ancient history. From another, this was the most significant human life that has ever been lived. It was the one human existence that fully satisfied God's expectations from human beings. It was the human life that restored God's order in creation and that offered a new worth and meaning to all those who would accept a share in it. It wasn't just what happened to Jesus that gave meaning to his life. It was how he dealt with what happened that was important, the meaning it acquired from his dedication to the love of the heavenly Father.

Thinking Catholic means looking on the events of our human existence with the proper perspective. Not much that happens to us is of irreversible importance. For the person who thinks Catholic, life is too short and too involved with more significant matters to spend much attention on things that other people may find important.

That's why laughter is a prominent dimension of thinking Catholic. Laughter is the human response to the incongruous, the unexpected, the disproportionate. We laugh when we are able to see the little side of supposedly big things. People who think Catholic are likely to laugh a lot.

This is not to say that thinking Catholic involves an ongoing state of mindless merriment, of laughing off everything. No, the kind of spiritual maturity that is expressed in thinking Catholic does see importance in the happenings of our life. Human successes and human hurts are not simply insignificant. Those who think Catholic have to come to grips with suffering and failure. But they see these things as temporary and as part of a whole. These things are not the last word, the final determinant of the worth and direction of our lives. They are merely episodes in the drama that constitutes a human existence, sometimes tragic episodes, sometimes episodes of comic relief. Even if the significance of the episode is not immediately clear, those who think Catholic know that the drama as a whole is going to have a happy ending. Everything has to be seen in relationship to that ending.

Jesus tells his disciples that if they seek first the Kingdom of God, everything else will fall into place (see Matthew 6:33). He doesn't say that everything else is meaningless, but secondary, relative to the principal action. Seeking the Kingdom means being open to the goodness and love that God offers us in Christ as the fundamental element of our life. Nothing else is equally important. Everything else derives its importance from its relationship to God's love and care for us.

Thinking Catholic means seeing the significance of what is really significant and seeing the relative insignificance of everything else. It all depends on that.

CHAPTER SEVEN

Sinners All

Every Catholic knows the Hail Mary. It's a prayer we say frequently, and every time we pray it we remind ourselves of what we are: "Holy Mary, mother of God, pray for us sinners...." We are sinners, each and every one of us.

Sin plays a significant part in thinking Catholic. We know that we are born into original sin. We are not associated with God at the beginning of our lives as our first parents were at the beginning of creation. Something is missing in us that they had, something they lost when they tried to take over God's role as host in the celebration. In addition, there is the sinfulness in the world around us, sinfulness so easy for us to learn to imitate. Then there are our own sins, big ones and small ones, the bad things we have done and the good things we have deliberately left undone. Each of us in his or her own way, to a greater or less extent, has played Adam and Eve in our relationship with our heavenly Father. Being aware of sinfulness is part of being Catholic. We know that what the author of the First Letter of John told the early Christians also applies to us: "If we say, 'We are without sin,' we deceive ourselves, and the truth is not in us" (1 John 1:8).

There is a whole branch of theology concerned (at least in part) with sin: moral theology. Catholic moral theologians over the centuries have studied sin and classified it and evaluated its various manifestations. They have analyzed the conditions that lead to sin and the various requirements of understanding and will that contribute to the gravity of sins. There isn't much about sin that hasn't been studied by Catholic thinking.

Given all this, it might seem that thinking Catholic demands an ongoing state of conscious guilt, a consistent awareness of failure and incompleteness. But that's only one aspect of thinking Catholic about sin. The Catholic mind-set also includes an awareness of God's desire to pardon, to forgive, to express his ongoing love and care for us in spite of our real and serious deficiencies.

That's why Catholic thinking about sin always includes the Sacrament of Reconciliation, that unique encounter between God, the Church and the sinner in which the individual expresses his or her guilt and, through the agency of the Church, receives forgiveness from God. Sin is an integral part of thinking Catholic, but so is God's mercy and love. You can never have one without the other if you are really thinking Catholic.

There are other ways to approach human sinfulness. One is to say there is no such thing. The idea that certain kinds of human behavior are inherently wrong and necessarily harmful to those who engage in them is outmoded. We may need human laws to keep antisocial behavior under control, but as long as what we do doesn't harm other people, we don't need to be concerned about it. The idea of sin is an attempt to keep people from doing what comes naturally to them. This approach to sin is quite common in the crazy world around us.

Another approach is to see our sinfulness as so deeply rooted and so much a part of our lives that there really isn't anything we can do about it. We can only acknowledge ourselves as totally powerless from the beginning and hope that God won't be as hard on us as we deserve when our life is over.

Both approaches are kinds of denial. The first denies that sin is real and is harmful and destructive to the sinner, apart from what it might do to other people. The second denies that God has any interest in what we do here and now. God simply allows us to go on sinning until the end, when, without any collaboration on our part, he either cleans up the mess we have made or writes us off completely.

Thinking Catholic denies nothing. It is quite clear about our sinfulness. Sin is real. It is common. It is ours. Each of us is born in detachment from God, and, even after God has united us with himself and his plans in Christ, we keep wanting to go off in other directions. None of us is particularly successful in playing the part that God has assigned to us in his celebration of goodness and love. We are too affected by the evil around us, too scarred by the wrong decisions we have made, too weakened by our own self-destructive acts and omissions. There's no way to deny that and still be in touch with sane reality.

But thinking Catholic is also realistic about God's response to our sinfulness. God never gives up on us. God loves us in spite of what we have done or not done.

God still wants us to participate in the celebration of creation. All he asks is that we acknowledge our sinfulness and accept once more his love for us. It's not that what we have done is not wrong or not destructive of God's handiwork in us. But God's love for us is greater than the greatest wrong we can inflict on ourselves or on God's good creation. We are all flawed merchandise, but God remains willing to have us anyhow.

Thinking Catholic about sin has a lot to be said for it. It teaches us that we don't have to pretend that we are not really sinners, that what we have done, in spite of the accusations of our heart, is not really bad, that everything is really all right, or somebody else's fault, or the result of forces within us that we simply can't control. Thinking Catholic about sin allows us to look ourselves directly in the eye and tell the truth about ourselves: We are sinners all. The best of us is infected by failure, and there is no way out of our plight except the free and ever-present love and mercy of God.

Thinking Catholic about sin also assures us that we don't have to achieve. God doesn't sit back to see what we are going to make of things and then, on the basis of what we have done with ourselves, determine whether or not we are worth anything. God knows from the beginning that none of us is worth much if left on our own, so he stands by us every step of the way, even when we are going off in the wrong direction. At the end, if we are still open to him in any way, he welcomes us into the Kingdom. What God welcomes is not the wonderful production that we have made of ourselves, but the result of the workings of his love on admittedly unpromising material.

If we are thinking Catholic we know that even our sinfulness is relative. It is not the last word unless we choose to make it so. It is not for that reason any less bad, destructive, rebellious, prevalent or real. It is simply not the whole picture. The whole picture has to include the love of the Creator for this self-seeking creature who finds it so hard to act responsibly. It has to include God's unlimited forgiveness and mercy for this so frequently unsuccessful production of his.

Thinking Catholic involves reassurance that God loves us in spite of our sins and confidence that, even though our life is not an unqualified success, it is still precious to God.

Thinking Catholic enables us to stand before the Lord with a smile of expectation, even as we acknowledge that we are sinners all.

CHAPTER EIGHT

Significant Others

Thinking Catholic is not done in the first person singular. It always involves the plural. It's not concerned with *me* but with *us*. While each of us is a unique individual, custom-made by the Creator and loved by God as the special persons we are, we never stand alone either in the sight of God or in the execution of our role in the celebration that is creation. Significant others are always included.

We all need other people to survive. Human beings are totally helpless when they are born. We need years of care before we can begin to think of existing without the hour by hour attention of our parents. And the care we need is not just physical. We have to be trained to walk and to speak, to act and to think. The values that motivate us and the goals we will pursue in our lives come to us almost exclusively from our family, at least until we reach a certain level of maturity. We simply cannot do without others.

That's why the family plays such a big part in thinking Catholic. Catholics are opposed to divorce and remarriage and to casual sexual activity not because Catholics are old-fashioned, but because they have an acute awareness of just how important the family is to the well-being of its members. How can children grow up to know about unconditional love and self-sacrifice if they grow up with confusing or destructive experiences of parenthood and family life? Our families make us what we are and, in spite of what our world seems to think, it is not likely that a truly healthy human being will grow and flourish in an unhealthy family.

But the significance of others does not lie just in what they can do for us. At a deeper level, the significance of others lies in what they are.

One of the most deeply held tenets of thinking Catholic is that each and every human being is valuable. Everybody is important. Everybody counts. From the rocket scientist to the wino in the gutter, from the pope to the war criminal, no human being can rightly be disregarded, written off, thrown away.

The reason we see worth in every human person is that every human person is part of God's creation, called to play his or her special part in the celebration of God's goodness and love. All human persons are precious to the Lord. If that were not so, they wouldn't be here. We may not be able to see or appreciate their worth, but that's not the issue. We are not in charge of the celebration, God is; and it is up to us to respect all the guests that God has invited to participate.

Given our dependence on others, given their own special value to God, it follows in thinking Catholic that we owe something to them. If we have been called to help God make the most of the celebration that constitutes creation, it is clear that the greatest share of our attention is owed to those others who have the most to contribute—God's human creatures. Because we share responsibility for creation, we share responsibility for one another.

We exercise this responsibility in many different ways. Parents exercise some of their responsibility through the love and care they give their children. Friends exercise responsibility in doing good for each other, in sharing burdens, in reflecting joys. We all contribute to the well-being of others by the work that we do, work that not only enables us to earn our living, but also provides goods and services that make the lives of other people better. Even in the small change of daily life we recognize the significance of others by the kindness and courtesy with which we treat them. We may not even know who they are, but they are important.

We also express our responsibility for others in the pursuit of social justice. The poor, the unsuccessful, even the lazy and the criminal are not disposable items that we can throw into the garbage can of society if they prove to be without immediate usefulness. They are God's creatures, each as unique and precious to God as we are. To marginalize them, to compel them to live in misery, to refuse to take them into account as we mold our society is to overlook and mistreat what God has called both them and us to be. To be significant to us doesn't require that the others attain a certain level of prosperity or success or usefulness. It requires only that they exist.

We are even called to love our enemies and do good to those who hate us. This command of the Lord is not just to challenge us or to spare us the self-destructiveness of hatred or to reduce conflict in the world. It's also to keep us aware that there is more to our enemy than his or her hostility to us and that that "more" has greater significance than the harm that we may experience at the enemy's hand.

It's easiest to extend ourselves for those we know best. We have received the most from them and our familiarity enables us to recognize the good that is in them. That's quite understandable. It's natural to love a neighbor. But we may not limit our concept of love of neighbor to response to the good that we receive or perceive.

One of the most memorable of Jesus' parables is the story of the good Samaritan (Luke 10:29-37), whose point is that the relationship of neighbor does not depend on religious or national affinity, but on need. The fact that the other may be different or strange or unknown or even bad is irrelevant. Whoever can benefit from what I have to offer is my neighbor, and it is that person to whom I owe my attention.

Thinking Catholic includes the conviction that nobody is permitted to be a loner in this life, to limit himself or herself to taking what is wanted or needed and leaving everybody else to look after themselves. We have all received too much for that. Our responsibilities for creation are too broad for that. The others are too significant for that.

All this responsibility is not meant to constitute a burden, a never-ending task of attending to the needs of countless others. It is rather an opportunity to become conscious of the grand spectrum of human variety, to accustom ourselves to looking for the good in others rather than for their usefulness to us, to appreciate the gifts that each person has to offer to the celebration and to be grateful for the gifts that we have to offer to them.

Jean-Paul Sartre, one of the atheist philosophers of our time, has said that hell is other people. Thinking Catholic says that heaven is other people, that our happiness and theirs is determined to a great extent by what we have to offer to each other. The celebration will not be complete without the full participation of each guest. We are all significant to God. God looks on each of us with love and delight. Thinking Catholic means learning to look on others with the eyes of God and to treasure people accordingly.

CHAPTER NINE

Having Isn't Happiness

The world in which we live runs on the presumption that the more people have, the more important they are and therefore the happier they are. The world pays the most attention to those who have most. Those who have lots of money and live in big houses and drive big cars are much more likely to have their words listened to and their wishes responded to than those who have less. They are the human success stories on which others look with admiration.

This crazy world keeps trying to persuade the rest of us that we, too, will be better off if we have more. That's why TV programs are written in ten- or twelve-minute segments: There will be more opportunities to sell things. The latest cars, the newest medications, the most stylish clothes, the best hammers and saws, the newest homes in the newest neighborhoods—insistently and persuasively we are told that we need these things, that we really can't get along without them, that having them will somehow make us happier. And once we have these things, we are told that's not really the end because now there are new and improved products that make the old ones obsolete. The implication in all of it is that our worth and our importance and therefore our happiness depend on what we have.

Obviously we have to have some things. We can't get along without food and clothing. We need some sort of shelter. In our increasingly complex world most people need their own means of transportation. If we want to stay in touch with what is going on around us we need radios and television sets. In these last few years it seems to have become necessary for even children to have a computer. We can't live with the same equipment that was sufficient for our grandparents.

There's nothing wrong with all that. God is pleased when we use the potential of his creation to improve our lives and make the best use of the capacities that he has put within us.

But possessions are dangerous. For one thing, they can be addictive. Something inside us seems to keep clamoring for more. We find it difficult to limit our possessions to what we need. It seems that everything we get requires us to get something more. In its extreme form, this inclination leads to the compulsive spending that even the world recognizes as a mental disorder. In its more ordinary manifestation, this inclination to possess leads us to acquire things that we don't really need, just for the pleasure of having them, and, once we have them, to put them aside and go after something else. How many possessions do we have that we never really use or even enjoy? How many of our possessions could we throw away or give to somebody else without noticing the difference? To some extent we are all possession junkies, hooked on irrational getting and having.

But even more dangerous than the pursuit of

possessions is the mentality that lies behind it. Our desire to have ever more is the expression of an inclination to make ourselves safe and independent, to surround ourselves with things so that we won't have to rely on anybody else, not even God, for our fulfillment. Implicit in the compulsion to have is the desire to set up our own little private celebration of life so that we won't have to bother with the celebration that God has invited us to. Apart from the radical discourtesy of such an attitude, it is also counterproductive. It won't bring us happiness, and it will deform our spirit.

The reason that possessions will not bring us happiness is that we are created for something else. God did not make us to latch onto things and to find our worth in what we have. God made us to participate in the ongoing celebration of creation, to make our particular contribution to the expression of his goodness and love, to want and to do good for those around us, to collaborate in his ongoing kindness and love. That's how we were meant to spend the years of our earthly existence, and only that can bring us fulfillment, only that can make us happy. If we direct ourselves to something less than that, if we try to find fulfillment in surrounding ourselves with secondary things like possessions, we are doomed to frustration, and, when the time comes to leave our possessions behind, we will find that our life has brought us only emptiness.

It's not just at the end that our possessions will betray us. They also deform us along the way. If we determine our value by what we have, we will soon find ourselves looking on other human beings as objects to be possessed rather than as significant others to be loved and respected. We will use people for our own purposes, and, once those purposes have been fulfilled, we will abandon them and look for others who can contribute in other ways to our personal enrichment. If things are the center of our lives, even human beings will become things for us.

But there's more. Our lives are governed and directed by the values and goals we espouse. What we want determines who and what we are. If we want lots of things, then those things govern and direct our earthly existence. Possessions are no longer instruments we use for a higher purpose; they become ends in themselves that take over our life. Instead of possessing our possessions, we will find that our possessions possess us.

Two manifestations of thinking Catholic call for special mention in this context of having and using. The first is vowed poverty. Within the community of the Church are religious under vows who have promised the Lord that they will be as detached as possible from possessions. Their vow of poverty does not mean they live in misery or want, but that they own nothing for themselves and will use only that portion of the world's goods that is necessary for the work they do. Far from being depressed because of what they do not have, they generally find a great sense of freedom in their poverty. These vowed men and women religious may seem to the world to be marginally mad because of all the wonderful things they have given up. But to those who think Catholic they are a source of encouragement and a sign of sanity.

The other manifestation of thinking Catholic in this

context goes by a name that we have recently begun to borrow from our Protestant brothers and sisters, although the kernel of it goes back to the teaching of Jesus. It is stewardship. Stewardship is a consciously developed awareness that what we possess we have on loan, that what we have been given has been given for God's work, that our own wants and needs have to be evaluated in the light of the needs of others, and that happiness does not consist in having a lot but in using wisely what we have. Stewardship is not some new gimmick that priests have thought up to increase Sunday contributions. It is rather a formula for sanity.

Thinking Catholic does not mean doing without possessions, but using what we have with care and gratitude to further God's purposes in creation. Those who think Catholic do enjoy the good things of the world, but they know that these things are only temporary and that they must be directed toward something beyond our individual satisfaction. Those who think Catholic use their possessions with detachment and with caution because they know how dangerous they can be. Above all, they know that happiness is not the same as having.

CHAPTER TEN

Friends of Jesus

We have seen that thinking Catholic is not a solitary exercise. Thinking Catholic is necessarily interpersonal and relational. One interpersonal relationship has a unique importance in the life of believers. It is our friendship with the Lord Jesus.

Some people look on Jesus only as a historical figure, a blip on the screen of the human drama, a dreamer who was put to death by his enemies because he just didn't fit in. Others look on Jesus as a great teacher, a man who told other human beings about God from his point of view and invited them to share in his ideas. Still others see Jesus as a stern lawgiver who told us what God demands of us and who promised to come back to judge each of us according to the way we listened to what he had to say.

Those who think Catholic look on Jesus primarily as a friend. Friends are those who love each other, who see the good in the other and who want to do good for the other. A friend will appreciate the good qualities of a friend and will be willing to overlook his or her limitations. Friends spend time together, not just doing things that both enjoy, but also sharing with one another what has happened since they last met—their successes and their frustrations, their dreams and their fears. Sometimes it is enough just to be in the company of our friends, without doing or saying anything at all. Friends are people who share themselves, not for any specific purpose, not for gain or profit, but simply because they are friends.

Jesus was big on friendship. He had a circle of followers who traveled with him and listened to what he had to say. He taught them as friends (see Luke 12:4). He called them his friends because he shared with them what he had come from the Father to bring to us human beings (see John 15:15). Their friendship was based on their willingness to listen to and follow what Jesus taught (see John 15:14).

When he was about to be done to death for his faithfulness to his heavenly Father, Jesus spoke about laying down his life for his friends and about how this was the greatest thing that one person could do for another (see John 15:13). And when one of his closest associates brought Jesus' enemies to where he could be arrested without resistance, Jesus nonetheless addressed him as friend (see Matthew 26:50). Jesus died for friendship.

Jesus' friendship was not limited just to this close circle of disciples. He had time for all sorts of people: for women of uncertain reputation (see Luke 7:39), for the poor and the disabled (see Mark 1:32 and following), for ordinary people who seemed to lack direction in their lives (see Matthew 9:36). He was even at ease in the company of those who were collaborating with the Roman oppressors of his people and those who weren't particularly careful about religious observance. He became notorious as "a friend of tax collectors and sinners" (see Luke 7:34).

This taste for friendship did not end with Jesus' death. After he had been raised from the dead, his first concern was to get back in touch with his friends (see Mark 16:7). He was patient with their uncertainty about who and what he was (see Luke 24:36 ff.). He explained to them the significance of what had happened to him (see Luke 24:26 and following). And with poor Peter, the boastful coward who had promised Jesus undying loyalty and then refused to admit that he even knew him, Jesus took special pains. He got Peter to acknowledge no less than three times that he still loved him, and then lovingly put him in charge of his flock. Their friendship was sealed by forgiveness (see John 21:15 ff.).

Then came the time when Jesus' earthly mission was over. He didn't say good-bye to his friends as if he were going away from them. Friends like to stay together, and Jesus' last words to his friends were, "And behold, I am with you always, until the end of the age" (Matthew 28:20). The friendship had not ended. It had merely entered a new phase.

Thinking Catholic means sharing in that friendship that Jesus promised would last to the end of time. Thinking Catholic means being friends with Jesus.

Catholics acknowledge Jesus as truly God, begotten of the Father before all ages, one with the Father and the Holy Spirit. Jesus is the Word of the Father, the expression of the Father's will for all creation, past, present and future. At the end of time Jesus will come to judge the living and the dead and our eternal destiny depends on the degree to which we have listened to and obeyed his commands.

But with all that, Jesus is still our friend, one who knows us and loves us as we are and who wants to do good for us. Jesus wants to be our principal friend, the One with whom we are more closely associated than with anybody else. If the story of each of our lives is the story of our participation in God's celebration of goodness and love, it is also the story of our relationship with Jesus.

Relationships demand contact, and friendship with Jesus means living in his company. Thinking Catholic means an ongoing awareness of the presence and the love of Jesus, not as a distant figure from the past, but as one near and real to us. When Jesus said he would be with his friends till the end of time, he meant that he would be with *us*. We never have to be alone, because the greatest friend we can ever have is always near.

This is not to say that everything we say and do is acceptable to Jesus. Real friendship does not call for approval when friends do something silly or harmful to themselves or to others. Friends owe it to one another to relate in truthfulness, and sometimes one friend has to say unpleasant things to the other. Our friendship with Jesus can be demanding, not because Jesus is looking for something for himself from us, but because he is looking for what is best for us.

Sometimes Jesus' friendship with us involves forgiveness, as it did with Peter. Our inherited inclination to sin and our chronic shortsightedness often bring us to abuse the friendship and the presence of Jesus. It is possible for us to go so far astray that we don't even want his friendship anymore. But that doesn't mean it's over. It only means that, when we turn back to Jesus, he is there as always, assuring us that he loves us in spite of what we have done.

Who and what we are is reflected by the kinds of friends we have. Thinking Catholic means treasuring and cultivating a lifelong friendship with the One who offered his life for his friends, who went out of his way to give comfort to those in pain and who paid attention to people that everybody else had written off. Being friends with Jesus gives a special dimension to our participation in God's work of creation here and now. Being friends with Jesus now also teaches us what we have to look forward to when we come finally into God's Kingdom.

Thinking Catholic means being at home with the presence of the Lord.

CHAPTER ELEVEN

Keeping in Touch

Some people look on prayer as something like the visits to Santa Claus that children make. It's not something that happens regularly, but only at a special time. They climb upon the knee of the man in the white beard, inform him of their desires, and hope that, if they have been good enough, he will listen to them and they will get what they have asked for.

Authentic prayer isn't quite like that. It's not just asking. It's not just occasional. And getting a response doesn't depend on how good we have been. Prayer is our conscious attentiveness to the presence of our friend Jesus, of his Father, of their Spirit who dwells within us. Prayer is consciously spending time with God. Prayer is the way we keep in touch with the Lord.

There are all kinds of ways to pray. Sometimes we use formulas out of prayer books or from our memory. These formulas give us direction about how to communicate with the Lord if we're not quite sure what to say to him. If we are tired or distracted they help us focus our attention. They are useful when Christian believers pray together. Over the centuries the psalms have been counted among the standard prayer forms for the Church.

Sometimes when we pray we use our own words in a kind of formal conversation. Maybe we make a visit to the Lord in the Blessed Sacrament and just tell him how things are going with us. Maybe we thank him in the morning for the hours that lie ahead of us, or praise him in the evening for his help and presence through the day. Sometimes we need to ask the Lord for things, for help with a problem, for patience with a difficult person or for courage in suffering. Sometimes we need to apologize to the Lord when we have turned away from him or neglected him. When we pray in these ways, explicitly taking time out to chat with God, we deliberately shut out the noise of the world around us and try to give our full attention to the Lord. It's like sitting ourselves down with a friend for some serious conversation.

But there are other ways to be in touch with the Lord, more informal and casual ones. Just acknowledging the presence of Jesus when we are waiting for the traffic light to change is prayer ("Lord, I know you are with me"). So is the nod in his direction when something nice happens to us ("Thank you, Jesus!") or the quick call for help in time of urgency ("Lord, help me get there on time!"). This is the sort of prayer that I think Saint Paul had in mind when he told the early Christians to pray constantly (see 1 Thessalonians 5:17 and Ephesians 6:18).

It may well be that the depth of our attentiveness to the Lord is expressed as much by these spontaneous encounters with him as by the number of words we say out of a book or by the amount of time we spend in formal sit-down sessions, assuming that what we communicate with him in these informal ways is sincere and not just religious words we use to avoid less acceptable language. If nothing else, these quick and frequent outreaches to God insure that we don't look on God as a distant master but as a friend who is always with us.

Whatever forms of prayer we may use, it is important that our prayer be balanced. Catholic thinking over the years has identified four main things that we should pray about, four contexts in which we need to be attentive to the presence of our friend, the Lord.

The most obvious, and probably the most common, is prayer of petition, when we ask God for the things we need. We tell the Lord our needs not to inform him of what we are expecting nor to persuade him to give us his help. God doesn't require that of us. It's rather a matter of expressing our dependence on the Lord. Prayer of petition is one of the ways in which we acknowledge that we are God's instruments in the celebration of creation and that we can't carry out our parts properly unless he is there to help us. Prayer of petition also sensitizes us to recognize God's help when it has come to us. If we have not lifted up our needs to the Lord we are likely to think that they have been met from some other direction.

Thanksgiving is another context in which people need to pray. Thanksgiving is always appropriate because there is always something to be thankful for: a good day, a problem resolved, an unexpected blessing, even the ordinary things that those who are not attuned to prayer might take for granted: sunshine, rain, honeybees, a break in the traffic jam. Those who are really skilled in prayer can even be grateful for things that seem to be burdensome. They know that our creative and loving Father and his Son Jesus never send us anything that is exclusively bad. There is always a reason to be grateful.

Another main category of prayer is contrition. We have already seen that an awareness of our own sinfulness is a significant part of thinking Catholic. The prayer of sorrow, asking for forgiveness, is one of the ways in which we make explicit that awareness—not in order to punish ourselves or to instill a sense of worthlessness, but to remain conscious that God loves us in spite of our limitations. To neglect the prayer of contrition is either to forget that we are sinners, which is an exercise in denial, or to forget how much God loves us, which is an exercise in self-destruction.

Then there is the prayer of praise, when we simply acknowledge how good God is, how creative, how generous, how merciful, how understanding, how patient, how providential. The prayer of praise is not complimenting God so that he will remain kind to us, a sort of self-interested flattery. The prayer of praise is a way in which we keep ourselves conscious of the kind of creation in which we live and the kind of Lord who is in charge of it. God doesn't need our praise. We need to praise God so that we don't forget who and what we are, so that we remain aware of what we are here for, so that we will be ready to join in the unending chorus of praise to which God calls us in the Kingdom.

Within the community of the faithful are men and women who dedicate their whole lives to prayer. They are the contemplatives, such as Trappists or Poor Clares.

Their purpose is not to get away from it all and avoid the burdens of ordinary life. Rather their purpose is to spend themselves in the highest activity of which human beings are capable, immediate and ongoing contact with God. In the process, they remind the rest of us of the purpose of prayer and keep us aware of what a wonderful and blessed thing it is to stay in touch with the Lord. They are the virtuosos and the teachers of prayer.

Prayer is not one more obligation that God has imposed on us, another chore in addition to doing good and avoiding evil. Prayer is a rich and varied exercise of conscious association with the Lord. It is a diet that keeps us strong and lively, vigorous in our execution of the part in creation that God has assigned to us, grateful for his unceasing gifts, confident in his ongoing presence. We need prayer for our spirits as much as we need food for our bodies.

The Lord is the source and goal of everything we are and of everything we aspire to. It's important for us to keep in touch. Thinking Catholic means being persons of prayer.

CHAPTER TWELVE

The Whole Picture

The word *catholic* means whole, entire, universal. We Catholics are part of a family community that extends throughout the whole world, that teaches the entire message of Jesus and offers the entire range of gifts that Jesus intended for his followers, that somehow embraces the universal history of humankind. Thinking Catholic means being aware of these dimensions of our relationship with God.

But thinking Catholic also involves a particularly "catholic" way of looking at the world in general. It is an inclination to see things not as isolated phenomena in the vast complex of creation and human history, but as a single, organized plan. It is an inclination to see the parts in relation to the whole picture. There is an all-embracing perspective in thinking Catholic.

This tendency to look at the whole picture is a consequence of the Catholic Christian belief about creation. That which surrounds us in the world is not the outcome of chance happenings over millions of years, but rather the unfolding of the single program of God's desire to share his goodness and love. It all arises from a single source and is all directed toward a single purpose. It's all part of the one celebration. It all hangs together in a single fabric of consistency.

Thinking in terms of the big picture is also a consequence of the Catholic Christian belief about redemption. When God became a human being in Jesus, the whole world entered into a deeper relationship with God. The world is no longer just a product of God's creative will. It is also the place where God actually lived as a human being long ago and where God still lives today in the ongoing life of Christ. Every aspect of it has been touched by the one Redeemer, and every facet of it will be united and preserved when the Redeemer's Kingdom comes in its final fullness.

When those who think Catholic look at creation and its source and purpose in this way, it is not some sort of abstract philosophical exercise. It is the expression of a mind-set that seeks to grasp the fullness and the coherence of creation and redemption in order to acknowledge and praise the goodness and wisdom of the Lord. In the final analysis, the Catholic worldview is an exercise in appreciation.

In the history of Catholic thinking there are many examples of this endeavor to see the whole picture. One of the most significant is the *Summa Theologicae* (Summary of Theology) of Saint Thomas Aquinas. This "summary" runs to about 3,200 pages of small print in double columns. It is primarily concerned with the study of God: God's nature, God's plan for our salvation and the execution of that plan through redemption by Christ, God's care for us in the Church, God's plans for us at the end of time. But it also deals with the meaning of creation, both visible and invisible, with human morality and the way we work as rational creatures, with prayer and vice and virtue. The *Summa* of Saint Thomas is an immense grid on which there is a place to position just about everything one could imagine, including branches of knowledge that have developed since Saint Thomas wrote. Saint Thomas's *Summa* is one of the masterworks of thinking Catholic, but it is only one of dozens of such works that Catholic thinkers have produced.

A more modern example of looking at the whole picture is the *Catechism of the Catholic Church*, which was published in 1994. Here the Church presents the fullness of its teaching as expressed in the Creed, in the sacraments, in the Ten Commandments (viewed as an expression of our life in Christ) and in the Our Father (viewed as the basic pattern for Christian prayer). It is not a collection of miscellaneous propositions or a laundry list of teachings, but rather a coherent and complete view of the way things are, organized to show that it all fits together in a single picture.

The *Catechism of the Catholic Church* does not deal with each and every conceivable bit of human knowledge, any more than Saint Thomas's *Summa* does, but, as expressions of thinking Catholic, both works provide a context in which everything fits somewhere or other. Fruit flies and supernovas, the laws of economics and of subatomic particles, the history of twelfth-century China and the poetry of Shakespeare—none of this is irrelevant to God's plan of creation and redemption. None of it is foreign to thinking Catholic. It all belongs somewhere in the big picture.

But seeing the whole picture is not something that is confined to big books. It also takes place in the ordinary life of those who think Catholic.

As believers we know that each one of us has been called to further God's purposes and that each of us fits somewhere in God's plan. None of us is unimportant or expendable. Similarly, the events of our lives, sad ones and happy ones, all make their contribution to what God has in mind for us. Nothing happens by chance. Even sins can be turned to a good purpose by our almighty Father. And those parts of our lives that we simply can't understand are not for that reason outside the big picture. They are simply signs that God's ways are not our ways. Christian faith in divine providence involves an awareness that there is one carefully planned scheme of things, that we are part of that scheme and that all creation is somehow connected with us in bringing it to completion.

This concern with the whole picture is one of the driving forces of Catholic education. Learning about our faith is not just a matter of "religion" and "morality." It also involves learning the what and the why of creation as a whole. Nothing is foreign to Catholic education simply because nothing is foreign to us—or to God.

The world around us is often suspicious of big pictures. Some hold that there is no one big picture. Others believe that, if there is, it is so far beyond our understanding that it is irrelevant to us. The culture in which we live is much more comfortable with a narrow focus, a focus that is directed principally to me, to my needs, to my wants. The rest of humankind is of no concern to me. The rest of creation is only meaningful to the extent that it is useful to me.

Such a narrow focus is unfortunate because it

excludes so much understanding and goodness and beauty and joy. People who see things this way prefer to spend their lives picking over the hors d'oeuvres instead of sitting down at the main table with the other guests at the celebration.

Thinking Catholic means being concerned with the whole picture, because the whole picture is the context in which we are called to be and to live. Ever since creation and, even more, ever since the Son of God became part of creation as a human being, there is no aspect of what is that is alien to God and to God's family. The interior life of God, Father and Son and Holy Spirit, God's goodness and love, God's mercy, God's plan, human history from beginning to end, human society, human health, human achievement in the arts, the realms of animals and plants and minerals, the vast sweep of the skies whose extent we are just beginning to learn: It's all part of the picture that God wants us to understand and appreciate and enjoy. Thinking Catholic means thinking big. It means thinking universal.

CHAPTER THIRTEEN

Called Into Christ Together

The Catholic Church means different things to different people. To some who are not its members the Catholic Church is the anti-Christ, a usurper that proclaims false teaching about Jesus. To others the Catholic Church is an interesting historical curiosity, a remnant of the past whose contemporary significance is confined to offering contrast to more enlightened modern ways of thinking. To others the Church is just one more religious organization put together by people who happen to share the same set of beliefs.

Even Catholics have different ways of looking on the Church, depending on which aspects of it they choose to emphasize. Most Catholics look on the Church with affection as a community in which they find comfort. Some look on the Church with anger because of what they have suffered at the hands of its representatives. Some like to concentrate on the Church around us as the Church militant, valiantly struggling to be faithful to the Lord and to defend itself against its enemies as it moves forward to its final triumph. Some like to view the Church as a preacher of social justice or as a stern teacher of unchanging doctrine. Some use images when they think of the Church: the people of God, the flock of Christ, the holy mother, the field full of good grain interspersed with weeds. All these ways of looking on the Church have some merit, because the Church is, in fact, complex: a collection of saints and sinners, a fabric of successes and failures, a reality too intricate to be fully expressed by a single image or a single idea.

Certain elements, however, must be included in any adequate grasp of the Church. First of all, the Church is about Christ. It is the continuation of the life and mission of the Lord Jesus. Next, the Church is composed of people who have been called to it by the Lord. The Church is not an organization put together by human beings to preserve the memory and the teaching of Jesus, but a gathering of men and women who have been called by God through Baptism to participate in the ongoing life of Christ. Finally, the Church is not a collection of individuals, each relating to the Lord on a one-to-one basis, but a community of believers interacting with each other and with Christ in the context of the world. The Church is the body of those called into Christ together.

There is no denying that there are problems and limitations in the Church. Not all those who are called into Christ together are faithful to their calling. Not all those who speak and act in the name of the Church are everything they should be. The Church reflects the constraints of human history, so that some things the Church did in the past now seem inappropriate from the perspective of the present. But all this, real as it is, is merely static in the Church's transmission of its message.

Thinking Catholic involves acknowledging and accepting the Church in its full reality.

In and through the Church Christ makes us holy in his Spirit. Every stage of life is touched by the love and the life of the Lord through his sacraments: Baptism that gives us birth, Confirmation and the Eucharist that offer us maturity and strength, Reconciliation and the Anointing of the Sick that deal with our moral and physical weaknesses. It's all part of God's plan to make us holy as Christ is holy.

In and through the Church Christ teaches us. Christ teaches us about the world and our part in it, about the significance of our life, about the Father's love for us, about what the Father has in store for us when our earthly life is over. Christ teaches us about the worth and dignity of other people and about the dangers of getting too involved with what surrounds us. Christ teaches us that, in the last analysis, he is the unifying power that brings everything together into one and gives significance to all that is.

And all this happens in the context of our togetherness in him. Christ makes us holy through the agency of his ordained priests. Christ teaches us in the context of our families, miniature churches established by the Sacrament of Matrimony, and then through other teachers who speak in his name. Christ sanctifies and teaches and cares for us through others in less formal ways, too. The love that believers show to other people is the love of Christ. The example of dedication, commitment, sacrifice and prayer that believers offer to those around them is not pious posturing but the simple expression of what friendship with Christ is all about. It constitutes tacit teaching. Christ has determined to lead us into an ever deepening relationship with himself through the life and action of those in whom he lives and acts. We need each other because it is in each other that we encounter the Lord. And unless we encounter the Lord, our lives are without meaning.

The Church has been around for a long time, and so we have an extended and rich family history. It includes those members we call saints (starting with Mary, the mother of Jesus) who have been conspicuously faithful and generous in their response to the Lord's call. It also includes other members of whom we are less proud.

Our family history includes official rituals and personal devotional practices, some dating from the times of the apostles, some from the imperial court of Byzantium, some from the Middle Ages, some from just a few years ago. Every era of the Church makes its contribution to the way in which we express the relationship that Christ has established with us.

Our family history includes a highly articulated body of teaching that reflects and clarifies and develops the teaching of Christ as it has been received and applied over the centuries. It involves thinkers and scholars such as Augustine and Dante and Newman, Julian of Norwich and Teresa of Avila, who have shared with the Church their insights about God, about the order of the world, about prayer, about what it means to be a friend of Jesus. Each has made the riches of Christ available to the community of the faithful in his or her particular way.

It's all part of the Church, yet it all reflects the same basic reality of being called into Christ together.

The Church expresses its nature most eloquently in the Sunday celebration of the Eucharist. Here is a gathering of people who have been reborn into the life of Christ. Some are fervent believers. Some are lukewarm. Some aren't sure why they are there at all. Yet they are together in the Lord. And at their gathering they hear the call of the Lord as the Lord offers it to them in sacred Scripture and as it is applied to the here and now by the Lord's priest. They express their acceptance of the Lord's teaching in psalms and hymns. Then they offer themselves to their heavenly Father in conjunction with the offering of faithfulness that Christ made on the cross. In response to their offering, Christ gives them himself in Holy Communion, to deepen his life in them and to strengthen them to carry that life with them into the often crazy world in which they live.

For those who think Catholic, Sunday Mass is not just an obligation to be fulfilled. It is a gift, an opportunity to be in touch with the Lord and to be in touch with one another. It is a source of light and energy and joy. It's something we need in order to stay aware that the real worth of our life consists in being called into Christ together.

The Church is old and new, comforting and frustrating, demanding and reassuring. The Lord calls us to embrace it all. Thinking Catholic means being in love with the Church.

CHAPTER FOURTEEN

Learning

L earning is something we do all the time. Recently some people I was with were talking about our public schools. One man said that it's wrong to blame the schools for all the difficulties of our society because the schools have access to the students for only about six hours a day for one hundred and eighty days a year. They teach as well as they can, but for all the other hours of the day and for all the other days of the year the students are being taught—and learning—elsewhere. They learn from television, from their friends, from what they see and hear on the streets in their neighborhoods. Schools provide only some of the learning. Most of what students learn comes from elsewhere.

It's the same for the rest of us. We are all being taught and we are all learning all sorts of things all the time.

We all need to learn because practically nothing of what we need to know in order to live and function as human beings is instinctive. Most of this knowledge is acquired. Some is acquired unconsciously, as when we learn to speak our native language by listening and practicing at home as we grow up. Some is acquired consciously, as when we learn to ride a bicycle or use a computer. But learn we must.

It's no different with thinking Catholic. It's not something that comes to us automatically. We have to learn it.

The foundations of thinking Catholic come to many of us in our families. If we are lucky enough to be born into a family of those who think Catholic, we learn the fundamental lessons from our parents and our brothers and sisters. Our basic attitudes about the world, about God, about prayer, about the meaning of effort and suffering, about success and failure, about possessions, about the Church all come to us through our families. We learn most of these lessons unconsciously, just by watching and listening to those around us. But all these attitudes are learned, and somebody has to teach them to us.

As we grow to maturity, what we have learned in our families is both supplemented and tested by the wider world. We go to school. We make friends and find activities outside our family. Eventually we get a job. Sooner or later we are on our own. In all these circumstances we are learning. And what we are learning either strengthens or weakens what we learned at home.

But as we launch into individual independence, new challenges arise, new sets of circumstances that are different from what we may have known before. They may have to do with our work or with our personal relationships or with our ambitions. For most people, starting a family of their own presents whole new vistas of the unknown that have to be dealt with. And we have to learn how to deal with all these things. Our previous experiences, at home and elsewhere, may have taught us the principles, but now we are faced with how to apply the principles to these specific circumstances. We always need to learn.

And the learning never ends. Each stage of our lives presents new questions, new demands for learning. Some people who do well in school do not do well at their jobs. Some people who seem very successful in youth and middle age find themselves at a loss when old age sets in.

If we have learned the fundamentals of thinking Catholic at home, we at least have a foundation to build on. If we have not, then the task of acquiring sane and sound attitudes toward the world and the Lord and the meaning of our human life is more demanding. But, whatever our personal circumstances, thinking Catholic is something that has to be learned and something that we have to keep learning throughout our whole lives.

Thinking Catholic presupposes a certain fund of informational knowledge, truths about our heavenly Father and Jesus and the Church and the world and standards of behavior. But that's not enough. If we don't go beyond that, our faith will become irrelevant to what goes on in our lives day by day. Merely "knowing" that God loves us won't make much difference if we are unable to see what that means when we fail an exam or lose our job or get a promotion or fall in love with somebody.

In addition to basic information, thinking Catholic involves attitudes and habits, and these attitudes and habits have to be learned and practiced.

Probably everyone who thinks Catholic would give

his or her own list of attitudes and habits that contribute to maintaining faithfulness and sanity in the course of our lifetime. The little list that follows offers some of the things that I have found important in my own life.

Looking for the Lord. The handiwork of the creator is everywhere. The love of the Lord Jesus is everywhere. The action of the Spirit is everywhere. But we have to learn to see it, and in order to see it we have to become accustomed to looking for it. Those who think Catholic try to be attentive to the presence and action of God in every aspect of their lives—in the successes and the failures, in the joys and the sorrows. Whatever is going on, they ask themselves, "Where is the Lord in this?"

Responding to the Lord. God does not call on us to be spectators in our lives. We are participants, and in order to participate appropriately in our lives we have to respond to what the Lord asks of us. Thinking Catholic means looking at the circumstances in which we find ourselves—our individual circumstances and the larger circumstances of the world around us—and asking ourselves, "What does the Lord look for from me here and now?"

Being grateful to the Lord. If we are aware that the loving Lord is the principal actor in our lives and that the Lord is interested in us and in our world, then we will necessarily be inclined to thank the Lord. Somehow or another, God is always blessing us. Somehow or another, gratitude is always appropriate. "What can I thank the Lord for now?"

Nourishing the life of the Lord in us. Life involves

the expenditure of energy and energy needs to be replaced. We can't live our whole lives on the fund of faith and practice that we may have received in our childhood. We have to keep replenishing the fuel supply. This means a lifetime of learning about the Lord through Scripture and the teaching of the Church. It means regular participation in the celebration of the sacraments. It means consistent contact with other persons of faith. Our society is big on following a healthy diet. Thinking Catholic means being attentive to getting proper spiritual nourishment.

All this could be reduced to two basic requirements for thinking Catholic: reflection and prayer. Reflection means consciously looking at our lives from the perspective of the Lord. Reflection is particularly important in our time because there is so much noise and glitter in the world around us that we can easily lose track of what's important unless we are accustomed to looking beneath it all for the reality that lies at the heart of things. Prayer means lifting our selves and our lives and our brothers and sisters and our world up to the Lord, maintaining constant contact with the sources of meaning and energy.

None of this is automatic. None of it can be taken care of once and for all. Thinking Catholic is a habit, and habits are acquired by practice, by doing things over and over again, day after day, until they become second nature to us, and then continuing the practice so that the habits don't gradually get replaced by other less healthy ones.

Thinking Catholic is based on gifts that God gives

each of us. But it is also based on our own decisions and practice. It is something that has to be worked at and learned.

Learning goes on our whole life long, consciously or unconsciously. And if we are not learning to think Catholic, then we are learning something else.

Conclusion

We live in a crazy world. It is a world that makes promises of happiness that it can never deliver, a world in which many look on human life as a commodity to be used rather than a gift to be respected, a world that denies the reality of evil, a world in which the principal virtue is selfishness. It is a world that cannot look much beyond the here and the now, a world that can find meaning only in the satisfaction of immediate wants and needs. It's a crazy world. The craziness is all around us. There's no avoiding contact with it. Yet this is the world in which we are called to live.

The only way to avoid being infected by the craziness is to have different values and different goals—healthy, true and realistic ones, consciously and firmly held. What's needed is a whole different mind-set, a fundamentally different way of approaching the challenges and opportunities of each day. Anything less than that will not be enough to keep us faithful to what God has called us to be.

In these reflections I have described some of the many aspects of such a mind-set, which I have called "thinking Catholic." Another writer might have made a different selection or provided a different order of presentation. But all aspects of thinking Catholic have a common ground. When all is said and done, thinking Catholic means having faith.

In this context, "faith" is not a series of propositions we accept with our minds. Nor is it a kind of mindless assumption that somehow everything is going to turn out all right. It is rather an understanding of and a response to the way things really are, an understanding that involves deeply held convictions, a response that includes the gift of our very selves to an adventure whose origins and goals are beyond our own making.

Thinking Catholic means accepting what God has told us about himself and about us, that whole complex of revelation offered by Jesus and proclaimed by his Church. But what we accept is not merely intellectual information, as when we accept what the experts tell us about ancient history or the inner workings of the atom. What God offers us is not just interesting information but basic truth about who and what we are, where we have come from and where we are headed, truth about the significance of our corporate human past and about the value of every moment of the present—basic truth that helps us make sense of literally everything. God doesn't offer us only knowledge. God offers us meaning, and it is meaning that makes the difference between wisdom and madness.

Because what God offers us is not mere information, we cannot assimilate it with simple assent. For example, "I believe that there are three Persons in God" and "I believe that the battle of Waterloo took place in 1815" are not the same kind of material. Merely "knowing" what God reveals to us is not enough. We have to make it our own. We have to understand the significance of what God is teaching us.

This understanding that God offers us is not one more program that we can tune in to as we surf our way through life. It is something different and deeper, and it calls for a special kind of attention. Moreover, it is so rich and complex that in a whole lifetime of attentiveness we can only begin to grasp it. The conviction that accompanies real faith demands practice in looking for the Lord. It requires a consciously acquired habit of mindfulness. Meaning does not come easily.

But faith is more than understanding. It is also response. It means giving our hearts and minds to participation in the project for which God made the world, the project in which God has called us to collaborate. The response involves gratitude as we become ever more aware of God's presence and action in our lives. It involves patience as we try to tease out the significance of what is going on around us. It involves the joyful gift of our talents and our resources in executing the role that God has assigned to us. Above all, it involves love, the will to give back to God in proportion as God has given to us.

Like the discovery of meaning, the response to meaning also requires practice—a whole lifetime of it. As we grow in our awareness of the meaning of the Lord in our world and in our lives, we keep finding new ways, deeper ways, often more demanding ways in which to respond. Our response is much more than keeping a set of rules. It is rather learning to act consistently with who and what we are. As our awareness of who and what we are matures, so does our response.

Faith involves understanding and response, deliberately pursued and consistently practiced. That's the agenda that God has given us for our lives.

Just as our lives are God's gift to us, so is our faith. Left to ourselves, we have no way in which to find meaning in the apparent jumble of the world around us. Left to ourselves, we can make no fitting response. Just as it is the Lord who provides the revelation, so it is the Lord who enables us to grasp it and to answer it. Everything is gift.

To have and to practice faith, to understand the world and its meaning and our part in it, to grasp the value of my human life and of every human life, to be aware of the presence of God in what goes on within us and around us, to savor our relationship with Jesus and with the brothers and sisters of Jesus in the Church, to see how it all fits together in a coherent vision, to accept it joyfully and confidently as God's gift and plan for us, to respond to it all with love on our part even as it is offered with love on God's part: That's what thinking Catholic is all about.

A long time ago, soon after the Church began, Saint Paul wrote a letter to the Christians of Rome. It's a long and complicated letter, basically concerned with the meaning of faith. Toward the end of the letter is a long section about putting faith into practice. At the beginning of that section, Saint Paul urges his readers: "Do not conform yourselves to this age but be transformed by the renewal of your mind, that you may discern what is the will of God, what is good and pleasing and perfect" (Romans 12:2). This summons is also addressed to us.

Faithfulness in a crazy world is not easy. It never has been. It is not something that follows automatically from being a member of the Church or from knowing Church teaching. The renewal of our mind to which Saint Paul invites us requires attention and effort.

Yet faithfulness is not just an ongoing struggle against heavy odds. It is an enterprise of eager confidence. We are called to live in an awareness of the profound meaning that God has put into his creation and to respond energetically and enthusiastically to that meaning with the resources that God has bestowed on us so generously. We are called to deal with things the way they really are. That's what constitutes faithfulness. That's what constitutes sanity. That's thinking Catholic.